*Dedication:*

*To my beloved children, Mario (Teik), Bruna, Victor, and Bárbara, who are the inspiration and reason for my relentless pursuit of knowledge. You are my strength and motivation to share my ideas and experiences.*

*To my husband, José de Vasconcelos Filho, whose collaboration and support were crucial in creating this book. Your unwavering dedication and support are a precious gift in my life.*

*To my dear grandchildren, Davi, Vivi, and João Gabriel, who represent the continuity of our stories and the hope for a bright future. May this book inspire you to explore your passions and seek truth in all things.*

*To my sons-in-law and daughters-in-law, Nikolas Bucvar, Eduardo, Jana, and Jacque, who strengthen our family with their love, support, and valuable contributions.*

*I am grateful for being part of this journey and for sharing your enriching perspectives and experiences.*

*This is dedicated to all of you, my beloved family, with all my love and gratitude.*

*Katia Doria Fonseca Vasconcelos*

## INTRODUCTION:

Welcome To "UQ Course For Visionary Leaders: Lesson 1- Balancing Potentials."

This course is designed for leaders who aspire to elevate their leadership to new heights by exploring the principles of UQ (Universal Intelligence Quotient) and applying them in their daily practices.

In this learning journey, you will have the opportunity to discover how to balance your potentials and develop essential skills to become a visionary leader.

By mastering the principles of UQ, you will lead with confidence, creativity, and effectiveness, tackling complex challenges with innovative approaches.

During this lesson, we will explore the significance of balancing potentials in visionary leadership. You will learn how 360-degree vision, Resilience, Adaptability, Synchronicity, and Emotional Control can drive your performance as a leader, enabling you to make informed decisions, overcome adversities, and guide your team towards success.

Throughout this course, we will provide valuable insights, practical exercises, and specific guidance to help you develop your leadership skills. You will be challenged to reflect on your current approach, identify areas for improvement, and set goals for balancing your potentials.

This course is an opportunity for self-development and personal and professional growth. We are thrilled to accompany you on this transformative journey, where you will discover your potential as a visionary leader and learn to apply the principles of UQ in your daily life. Get ready to expand your horizons, develop key skills, and become an exceptional visionary leader.

This is just the beginning of an exciting and challenging journey. Embrace this opportunity for growth and get ready to become the visionary leader the world needs. We are prepared to walk beside you on this quest for excellence in leadership!

# TABLE OF CONTENTS

# UNDERSTANDING UQ PRINCIPLES

Human success is driven by the balance of UQ (Universal Synchronistic Intelligence Quotient), a concept backed by scientific research and case studies. Several studies have explored the aspects of UQ and its effects in different areas of human life.

A study conducted by researchers from Stanford University revealed the importance of developing resilience and emotional control in achieving positive outcomes in careers and relationships. This research demonstrated how the ability to cope with adversity and control emotions contributes to making sound decisions and building healthy and productive relationships.

Renowned Harvard Business School professor Clayton Christensen highlights that disruptive innovation requires a shift in approach and overcoming outdated paradigms. He emphasizes that success lies in embracing change and adapting quickly to new circumstances.

Psychologist and Nobel Prize-winning economist Daniel Kahneman reminds us that our decisions are influenced by how we frame problems. By adopting a positive perspective and seeing challenges as opportunities for learning, we can make more informed decisions and achieve superior results. The theory of emotional intelligence, developed by Daniel Goleman, also aligns with the concept of UQ, emphasizing the importance of emotional balance for personal and professional success.

Renowned psychologist and Harvard Graduate School of Education professor Howard Gardner emphasizes the importance of balancing and developing all of our intelligences. He encourages us to reprogram our educational approach, valuing not only logical-mathematical intelligence but also emotional, musical, spatial, and other intelligences, allowing us to explore our full potential.

These great minds, along with other advocates of innovative thinking, reinforce the importance of adopting a new perspective in the face of challenges. By balancing our potentials through 360-degree vision, resilience, adaptability, synchronicity, and emotional control, we will be prepared to face challenges with confidence, creativity, and effectiveness. This approach also relates to other relevant theories and concepts, such as Carol Dweck's growth mindset, which emphasizes the importance of a growth mindset in the pursuit of success.

In this course, we will comprehensively explore the principles of UQ and how they relate to different areas of human life. We will analyze scientific research, inspiring case studies, and relevant theories to provide a broad and informed view of UQ balance and its impact on personal and professional success.

Now, let's dive into the exploration of the five principles of UQ: 360-

degree vision, resilience, adaptability, synchronicity, and emotional control. Each of these principles plays a fundamental role in seeking balance and developing your potentials.

360-degree vision: 360-degree vision involves having a broad and comprehensive perspective on all dimensions of your life. It is the ability to see beyond the obvious, to understand the interconnections between different areas, and to identify opportunities that others may not perceive. In challenges related to 360-degree vision, you will be encouraged to explore different angles and consider various perspectives to make informed decisions.

Resilience: Resilience is the ability to cope with adversity, overcome obstacles, and quickly recover from challenging situations. It is the ability to adapt to change and keep moving forward, even in the face of difficulties. In resilience challenges, you will be challenged to confront difficult situations, learn from them, and find ways to strengthen yourself in the face of adversity.

Adaptability: Adaptability is the ability to adjust and adapt to different circumstances and demands. It is the capacity to be flexible, open to change, and willing to experiment with new approaches. In adaptability challenges, you will be challenged to step out of your comfort zone, try new ways of doing things, and adapt to changes in your environment.

Emotional Control: Emotional control involves the ability to manage your emotions effectively, especially in high-pressure and stressful situations. It is the skill of maintaining calm, making rational decisions, and dealing with challenges in a balanced manner. In emotional control challenges, you will be challenged to recognize your emotions, develop strategies to deal with them, and maintain emotional balance in challenging situations.

Synchronicity: Synchronicity refers to the harmony and coordination of your actions in the environment you are in. It is the ability to synchronize your tasks, projects, and goals to achieve an efficient and effective workflow. In synchronicity challenges, you will be challenged to organize your activities, set priorities, and find ways to optimize your time and resources.

Throughout this course, we will explore each of these principles in detail, presenting practical challenges, reflective questions, and exercises that will help you develop your skills and balance your potentials.

The UQ concept, Universal Synchronistic Intelligence Quotient, is an approach that aims to enhance intelligence and cognitive abilities through the balance of 360-degree vision, adaptability, resilience, synchronicity, and emotional control principles. It was conceived by a multidisciplinary team of experts in neuroscience, psychology, and management, led by renowned researcher and coach Katia Doria Fonseca Vasconcelos.

UQ was developed based on scientific foundations that prove the importance of balancing these principles in personal and professional development. Studies conducted by distinguished researchers such as psychologists Daniel Goleman and Daniel Kahneman emphasize the relevance of emotional control and a positive perspective in making sound decisions and achieving personal success.

The application of UQ as a metric and parameter occurs through the evaluation and monitoring of UQ principles in different areas of life. Self-assessment is a fundamental tool in this process, allowing individuals to identify which principles they need to develop and balance to achieve a higher level of intelligence and cognitive performance.

Balancing UQ potentials is essential for tackling

complex challenges. By balancing 360-degree vision, adaptability, resilience, synchronicity, and emotional control, the chances of finding effective solutions to problems increase significantly. This approach provides a broad and comprehensive view of challenges, enabling them to be faced with confidence, creativity, and effectiveness.

Developing potentials and achieving balance in UQ requires dedication, practice, and continuous self-development. It is a process that involves personal commitment to enhancing cognitive and emotional skills, as well as seeking appropriate knowledge and guidance to achieve better results in problem-solving and personal and professional success.

Prepare for a journey of self-discovery, personal growth, and full activation of your UQ!

Remember, balancing these principles is essential to achieve extraordinary results in all areas of your life. Let's explore, challenge, and develop the best in you. We are excited to accompany you on this transformative journey!

# INSTRUCTIONS FOR MANAGERIAL CHALLENGES

In this section, you will face a series of managerial challenges, each presenting a fictional and unique situation that requires your leadership skills. The challenges have been designed to test and develop your capabilities in various essential areas, including 360-degree vision, resilience, emotional control, adaptability, and synchronicity.

360-degree vision: In each challenge, you will be

invited to analyze the situation from different angles and consider various perspectives to make informed decisions. Be open to listening to the opinions and ideas of your team, colleagues, and other stakeholders before arriving at a solution.

Resilience: Resilience is the ability to deal with adversity, overcome obstacles, and quickly recover from challenging situations. In the challenges, you will encounter situations that require courage and determination to find solutions, even in the face of seemingly insurmountable obstacles.

Adaptability: Adaptability is crucial in an environment of constant change. In the challenges, you will need to adjust to new circumstances, embrace change, and experiment with new approaches. Be willing to step out of your comfort zone to find creative solutions.

Emotional Control: Leadership requires dealing with a range of emotions, both your own and those of others. Maintain calm and make rational decisions even in high-pressure and stressful situations. In the challenges, acknowledge your emotions and employ strategies to handle them in a balanced manner.

Synchronicity: Synchronicity involves harmoniously and effectively coordinating your actions with team activities and organizational goals. In the challenges, you will be challenged to optimize teamwork, prioritize tasks, and ensure that all activities are aligned to achieve objectives efficiently.

Instructions for the Challenges: Each challenge will present a specific situation that demands your leadership skills. Read the descriptions carefully and consider the above guidelines when facing the challenges. After each challenge, reflect on your decisions and approaches, seeking to improve your skills and learn from each experience.

Remember: Be open to learning and growing with each challenge. There is no one-size-fits-all or right answer for every situation, and the learning process is as important as the outcome. Be confident in your abilities and creativity as you are about to embark on a journey of UQ development and balance.

Ready to face the Managerial Challenges and expand your leadership skills? We are confident that you will succeed and thrive throughout this journey. Good luck, and may you grow into an even more efficient and capable leader!

## CUSTOMER SERVICE CHALLENGE

Carlos woke up early that morning, as usual, to take his children to school before heading to work. The morning routine was always hectic, and with his wife also working, they both had to share the responsibilities. However, that morning, things didn't go as planned. His wife, feeling under the weather and having slept poorly, forgot to prepare the kids' snacks, which led to a small argument between them before leaving the house.

When he reached the garage to get the car,

Carlos noticed a flat tire and had no choice but to leave the car at his parents' house and take the bus to work. Unfortunately, the bus was overcrowded, and he ended up arriving late, receiving a scolding from his boss as soon as he entered the office.

Despite trying to compose himself, the stress from the hectic morning was still present. Carlos started attending to clients over the phone, and some of them were friendly, which helped improve his mood. However, close to lunchtime, a customer called complaining about an erroneous charge, and

Carlos knew it was his responsibility to resolve the issue.

Unfortunately, his boss went out for lunch and left Carlos alone to deal with the irate customer. Carlos followed the standard customer service protocol, trying to calm the customer and explaining that he would resolve the issue. However, the customer became increasingly aggressive and wouldn't accept his explanations.

Carlos felt pressured and challenged. He tried to remain calm and use his emotional control skills, but the customer continued to be aggressive. He offered alternative solutions, but nothing seemed to satisfy the customer. When Claudio, his boss, returned from lunch, he was informed about the complaint from the same customer, claiming that Carlos treated him aggressively and hung up during the call. The customer called again, and another agent attended to him, but he demanded to speak with Carlos' supervisor to report the situation.

Now, putting yourself in Claudio's shoes to talk to Carlos, as a leader, you must handle the situation appropriately and efficiently. How would you approach Carlos to address the customer's complaint while also supporting him through this difficulty? As a leader, what would you do to resolve the situation in the best possible way and ensure Carlos' emotional well-being? Describe your approach and actions to face this challenge as a leader in the presented situation.

UQ Self-Assessment Test

## Dealing with Carlos' Situation - Boss Claudio's Perspective

Put yourself in the shoes of Boss Claudio and answer the following questions about how you, as a leader, would handle Carlos' situation, the customer service representative, after receiving the complaint from the aggressive customer:

360-degree vision:

How would you consider different perspectives when addressing Carlos about the customer's complaint?

a) Ignore Carlos' perspective and assume the customer is right without hearing his side of the story.

b) Listen to Carlos' version, but focus solely on the customer's perspective to resolve the issue.

c) Listen to both the customer's and Carlos' versions to have a complete view of the situation before making any decisions.

Resilience:

How would you handle the pressure of resolving the conflict between the customer and Carlos?

a) Get frustrated and take the pressure out on Carlos, blaming him for the customer's complaint.

b) Try to solve the problem quickly but without considering Carlos' emotional well-being.

c) Show resilience, understanding, and empathy, offering support to Carlos during the resolution process.

Emotional Control:

How would you maintain emotional control when addressing Carlos about the customer's complaint?

a) Express your irritation and frustration directly to Carlos, escalating the tension of the situation.

b) Attempt to calm yourself down, but still let your dissatisfaction with the situation show.

c) Keep calm and approach the situation with empathy, avoiding impulsive emotional reactions.

Synchronicity:

How would you coordinate your actions when dealing with the customer's complaint and at the same time supporting Carlos?

a) Prioritize a quick resolution of the complaint, even if it means neglecting Carlos' well-being.

b) Try to solve the customer's problem but forget to provide support to Carlos.

c) Coordinate your actions, offering support to Carlos while working to resolve the customer's complaint fairly.

Adaptability:

How would you adjust to the situation, considering that each employee has different needs and reactions under pressure?

a) Adopt an inflexible approach, expecting Carlos to deal with the situation on his own.

b) Try to adapt to the situation but without fully understanding Carlos' specific needs.

c) Be flexible and adaptable, offering personalized support to Carlos based on his individual needs.

Answer Key:
After answering these questions, evaluate the approach you would adopt when dealing with Carlos' situation as a leader and add up the points:
a: 0 points
b: 1 point
c: 2 points

Evaluate the approach you would adopt:

UQ 10% 0 to 5 points: You would face significant difficulties in applying the principles of UQ in leading Carlos in this situation, and you may need to improve your skills in some specific areas.

UQ 25% 6 to 8 points: You would demonstrate effort in applying the principles of UQ, but there would still be room for improvement in some leadership areas with Carlos.

UQ 100% 9 to 10 points: Congratulations! You would effectively apply the principles of UQ in leading Carlos in this situation, demonstrating solid skills in 360-degree vision, Resilience, Emotional Control, Synchronicity, and Adaptability.

I hope this self-assessment test helps you reflect on how you could apply the principles of UQ in leading Carlos during this challenging situation. By analyzing the test results, you can develop an action plan to improve your skills and be a more effective leader when facing challenges with your team.

# E-COMMERCE PROJECT CHALLENGE

João leads an e-commerce project with a team of 8 highly skilled collaborators. The project has been successful so far, but a new unexpected demand arises: a client wants the app developed by the team to be capable of controlling their 8 wholesale stores located in different regions of Brazil and one store overseas. This is a novel proposal for João and his team, as they have never faced such a complex project.

Additionally, João faces an additional dilemma. Two of the team members, Rita and Renata, have Autism Spectrum Disorder (ASD), but they have been highly productive and have made significant contributions to the project. However, due to their ASD conditions, drastic changes and new work approaches may affect them more than the other team members, and the deadline for delivering this new project is tight.

João now faces a difficult decision: hiring two new collaborators to specifically handle this new project, which could expedite the delivery, but would also require time for integrating these new members into the team; or investing in the training and development of Rita and Renata so that they can adapt to the new project format and contribute to its realization.

As the project leader, João needs to make the best decision to ensure the project's success, meet the client's expectations, and maintain the emotional well-being of his team, including Rita and Renata.

## Self-Assessment UQ Test:

### DEALING WITH THE LEADERSHIP DECISION IN THE E-COMMERCE PROJECT

Put yourself in João's shoes and answer the following questions about how you, as a leader, would handle the situation of collaborators Rita and Renata regarding the new project:

360-degree vision:

How would you consider different perspectives when deciding on the team for the new project?

a) Ignore Rita and Renata's needs and immediately hire new collaborators to meet the deadline.

b) Prioritize technical skills and experience and choose to replace Rita and Renata with new collaborators.

c) Take into account Rita and Renata's unique skills, as well as their special adaptation needs, and assess if it's possible to develop them for the project.


Resilience:

How would you handle the tight deadline and pressure to deliver the new project?

a) Become overwhelmed and transmit stress to the team, resulting in a tense atmosphere.

b) Try to meet the deadline at all costs, even if it means sacrificing the quality of work and the team's well-being.

c) Show resilience in facing the challenge and seek effective solutions that balance the deadline and team empowerment.

Emotional Control:

How would you remain calm and supportive while dealing with the anxiety and needs of Rita and Renata?

a) Express frustration and impatience regarding their adaptation to the new project.

b) Attempt to ignore Rita and Renata's emotional needs, focusing only on technical demands.

c) Demonstrate empathy and patience, providing emotional support and adaptation strategies to cope with changes.

Synchronicity:

How would you coordinate the team's actions to tackle this complex challenge and ensure a successful delivery?

a) Allow each team member to work independently without considering collaboration among them.

b) Assign tasks without concerning yourself with communication among team members.

c) Promote synchronicity, encouraging collaboration and knowledge sharing among all team members.


Adaptability:

How would you adjust to Rita and Renata's specific needs regarding the new project?

a) Make no adaptations and expect them to naturally adjust to the changes.

b) Attempt some adaptations but without truly understanding their individual needs.

c) Be flexible and adaptable, offering personalized support to meet Rita and Renata's needs, ensuring they have a conducive work environment for their productivity.

Answer key:
After answering these questions, evaluate the approach you would adopt as a leader to face this challenge with the e-commerce project team and add up the points:
a: 0 points
b: 1 point
c: 2 points

Evaluate the approach you would adopt:

UQ 10% 0 to 5 points: Your approach may need improvement in dealing with the emotional and adaptive aspects of the situation, seeking a balance between efficiency and team well-being.

UQ 25% 6 to 8 points: You would demonstrate effort in applying the UQ principles, but there would still be room for improvement in some areas of leadership with the e-commerce project team.

UQ 100% 9 to 10 points: Congratulations! Your approach as a leader reflects the effective application of the UQ principles to face the challenge with the e-commerce project team, demonstrating solid skills in 360-degree vision, Resilience, Emotional Control, Synchronicity, and Adaptability.

I hope this self-assessment test helps you reflect on how you could apply the UQ principles in leading the e-commerce project during this challenging situation. By analyzing the test results, you can develop an action plan to improve your skills and become a more effective leader when facing challenges with your team.

## CHALLENGE OF THE SENIOR MANAGER IN A SOCIAL NETWORKING PLATFORM

Rogério was hired to be the Senior Manager of a social networking platform undergoing significant changes. Users have been facing problems with bugs while generating content, resulting in a decrease in the number of platform users. To address these issues, the company implemented changes and hired new collaborators, as the previous team left many errors in the project.

However, some long-time collaborators remained on the team and are showing resistance to the changes proposed by Rogério. They feel envious for not being chosen for the Senior Manager position, believing they deserved the role due to the time they've been with the platform.

Rogério has a three-month probationary period to prove his effectiveness as a leader and resolve the platform's issues, but the resistance from the long-time collaborators is an additional challenge.

Now, placing yourself in Rogério's position as the Senior Manager, you must handle the situation appropriately and efficiently. How would you approach these collaborators to address their resistance to change and, at the same time, motivate them to collaborate with the new initiatives of the platform? Describe your approach and actions to face this challenge as a leader in the presented situation.

# UQ Self-Assessment Test

DEALING WITH RESISTANCE TO
CHANGE - ROGÉRIO'S
PERSPECTIVE, SENIOR
MANAGER

Put yourself in Rogério's shoes and answer the following questions about how you, as a leader, would handle the resistance to change from the long-time collaborators:

360-degree vision:

How would you consider the perspectives of the long-time collaborators when addressing resistance to change?

a) Ignore the perspectives of the long-time collaborators and impose your decisions without listening to their concerns.

b) Superficially listen to their perspectives but prioritize your own ideas and plans.

c) Actively listen to their perspectives, take their concerns into account, and involve them in seeking solutions.

Resilience:

How would you deal with possible negative reactions and criticisms from the long-time collaborators regarding the changes?

a) Become demotivated and give up on implementing the changes to avoid conflicts.

b) Try to convince the long-time collaborators to accept the changes, but feel discouraged by the criticisms.

c) Demonstrate resilience by persevering with the changes, even in the face of criticisms, and seek solutions to their concerns.

Emotional Control:

How would you maintain emotional control in the face of negative reactions from the long-time collaborators?

a) Express your frustration and irritation openly, which could worsen the situation.

b) Try to hide your emotions but still feel uncomfortable and under pressure.

c) Keep calm and approach the situation with empathy, avoiding impulsive emotional reactions.


Synchronicity:

How would you coordinate your actions to address resistance to change while also motivating the entire team to achieve the platform's objectives?

a) Focus solely on convincing the long-time collaborators, neglecting the other team members.

b) Implement changes without considering the concerns of the long-time collaborators, aiming only for immediate results.

c) Coordinate your actions in an integrated manner, involving the whole team in seeking solutions, and strive to keep the team united and motivated.


Adaptability:

How would you adjust to the situation, considering that some collaborators have difficulty dealing with changes?

a) Not worry about supporting the long-time collaborators, expecting them to adapt on their own.

b) Try to adapt, but not fully understand the specific needs of the long-time collaborators.

c) Be flexible and adaptable, offering personalized support and strategies to help the long-time collaborators cope with the changes.

Grading:

After answering these questions, evaluate the approach you would adopt as a leader to face this challenge with the e-commerce project team and add up the points:
a: 0 point
b: 1 point
c: 2 points

Evaluate the approach you would adopt:

UQ 10% 0 to 5 points: Your approach may need improvements to deal with the emotional and adaptive aspects of the situation, seeking a balance between efficiency and team well-being.

UQ 25% 6 to 8 points: You would demonstrate effort in applying the UQ principles, but there would still be room for improvement in some areas of leadership with the project team.

UQ 100% 9 to 10 points: Congratulations! Your approach as a leader reflects the effective application of UQ principles to face the challenge with the e-commerce project team, demonstrating solid skills in 360-degree vision, Resilience, Emotional Control, Synchronicity, and Adaptability.

I hope this self-assessment test helps you reflect on how you could apply UQ principles in leading the e-commerce project during this challenging situation. By analyzing the test results, you can develop an action plan to improve your skills and become a more effective leader in facing challenges with your team.

## Challenge of Manager Moisés at the Clothing Store

Moisés is the manager of a department in a clothing store at a shopping center and is facing difficulties with inventory control as several items have been disappearing from the store. Security cameras reveal that some people enter the store to try on clothes and leave without making any purchases, but the detection system has not shown any malfunctions or triggered the alarm when customers leave the store.

Concerned about the missing items, Moisés decides to take action and follows the protocol for such situations. He informs his superiors about the problem and receives guidance to conduct a thorough investigation. A trusted employee reveals that one of her colleagues from the morning shift has been leaving later than the others and always with a full bag. This report raises suspicions about this employee, and now Moisés needs to prepare to find out if she is the cause of the problem.

# UQ Self-Assessment Test

DEALING WITH STOCK ITEMS
DISAPPEARANCE - MOISÉS'
PERSPECTIVE, DEPARTMENT
MANAGER

Put yourself in Moisés'
shoes and answer the
following questions about
how you, as a leader, would
handle the challenge of
stock items disappearance:

360-degree vision:
How would you approach the situation considering the perspectives of the suspected employee and other team members?

a) Focus exclusively on the informant's information, disregarding the perspective of the suspected colleague.
b) Take the report into account, but not make an effort to understand the concerns of the suspected employee.
c) Listen carefully to both the reporting employee and the suspected colleague to have a comprehensive view before making any decisions.

Resilience:
How would you deal with the pressure of resolving the stock items disappearance issue?

a) Feel anxious and overwhelmed, which could hinder your actions and decisions.
b) Try to quickly resolve the problem without considering the importance of following the correct process.
c) Maintain composure and resilience, facing the challenge step by step and seeking effective solutions.

Emotional Control:
How would you maintain emotional control when confronting the suspected employee about the missing items?

a) Express anger and accuse the employee without giving space for explanations.

b) Try to hide your emotions, but still show irritation during the conversation.

c) Approach the situation calmly and empathetically, avoiding impulsive emotional reactions and offering space for the employee to defend themselves.

Synchronicity:
How would you coordinate your actions to conduct the investigation while keeping the team focused and motivated?

a) Invest all resources in the investigation, leaving the team without guidance and support.

b) Try to conduct the investigation without involving the team to avoid distractions.

c) Coordinate your actions, strategically involving the team so that everyone feels supported and motivated.

Adaptability:
How would you adjust to the situation, considering that the suspected employee may react negatively to the approach?

a) Avoid confronting the suspected employee to avoid conflicts.

b) Try to adapt, but not take into account the individual needs of the employee.

c) Be flexible and adaptable, seeking a personalized approach to deal with the suspected employee and their reactions.

Grading:

After answering these questions, evaluate the approach you would adopt as a leader to face the challenge of the missing stock items and tally the points:

a: 0 points
b: 1 point
c: 2 points

Evaluate the approach you would adopt:

UQ 10% 0 to 5 points: Your approach may need improvements to deal with the emotional and adaptive aspects of the situation, seeking a balance between efficiency and the well-being of the team.

UQ 25% 6 to 8 points: You would demonstrate effort in applying the UQ principles, but there would still be room for improvement in some leadership areas during the investigation of the missing stock items.

UQ 100% 9 to 10 points: Congratulations! Your approach as a leader reflects the effective application of the UQ principles to face the challenge of the missing stock items, demonstrating solid skills in 360-degree vision, Resilience, Emotional Control, Synchronicity, and Adaptability.

I hope this self-assessment test helps you reflect on how you could apply the UQ principles in leadership during this challenging situation. By analyzing the test results, you can develop an action plan to enhance your skills and become a more effective leader when facing challenges with your team.

## LEADERSHIP CHALLENGE AT THE GYM

Marina is the manager of a gym and fitness center belonging to a large chain, but it is a family-run business managed by the owner's relatives. Her unit is known for excellent customer service and a dedicated and well-prepared team. Everything is going well until her superiors communicate their intention to implement significant organizational changes, including doubling the number of team members. However, Marina knows that the current infrastructure cannot accommodate this change and decides to conduct a risk assessment to present to her superiors.

Due to her professional competence, Marina conducts a thorough analysis of the risks involved in the proposed changes and prepares a comprehensive dossier to present to her superiors. However, one of the business partners, who is the majority shareholder's sister-in-law, disagrees with

Marina's approach and takes the situation personally. She becomes upset with Marina's conduct and decides not to present the risk analysis dossier to the superiors, in addition to trying to undermine Marina's position within the company.

Now, placing yourself in Marina's position as the manager, you must handle the situation appropriately and efficiently. How would you approach the business partner who did not present the risk analysis dossier and is trying to harm your

position in the company?
Describe your approach
and actions to face this
challenge as a leader in the
presented situation.

## Self-Assessment UQ Test

DEALING WITH PERSECUTION
AND RESISTANCE - MARINA'S
PERSPECTIVE, MANAGER


Put yourself in Marina's
shoes and answer the
following questions about
how you, as a leader, would
deal with the persecution
and resistance from the
business partner.

360-degree vision:

How would you consider the partner's perspectives when addressing the situation of persecution and resistance?

a) Ignore the partner's perspectives and confront her directly, leading to more conflicts.

b) Try to avoid confrontations but not take into account the partner's concerns.

c) Listen attentively to the partner's perspectives and seek to understand her concerns to find a collaborative solution.


Resilience:

How would you deal with the partner's persecution and possible negative reactions to your approach?

a) Feel demotivated and consider giving up on the risk analysis and proposed changes.

b) Try to stand your ground, but feel discouraged by the negative reactions.

c) Demonstrate resilience and persistence in your actions, seeking solutions even in the face of negative reactions.

Emotional Control:

How would you maintain emotional control in the face of the partner's persecution?

a) Express your frustration and indignation with the situation, making the environment even more tense.

b) Try to hide your emotions, but feel shaken and under pressure.

c) Remain calm and approach the situation with empathy, avoiding impulsive emotional reactions.


Synchronicity:

How would you coordinate your actions to deal with the partner's persecution and, at the same time, continue presenting your proposals effectively?

a) Focus solely on confronting the partner, neglecting the progress of the proposals.

b) Try to proceed with the proposals, ignoring the persecution, even if it may negatively impact the presentation.

c) Balance your actions, facing the partner's persecution assertively while maintaining focus on the effectiveness of the presentation.

Adaptability:

How would you adjust to the situation, considering that you are facing resistance to the proposed changes?

a) Not worry about finding common ground with the partner, seeking to push forward with your proposals at any cost.

b) Try to adapt, but not take into account the partner's specific concerns.

c) Be flexible and seek strategies to find common ground with the partner, involving her in the decision-making process.

Grading:

After answering these questions, evaluate the approach you would adopt as a leader to face this challenge as a manager and add up the points:
a: 0 point
b: 1 point
c: 2 points

Evaluate the approach you would adopt:

UQ 10% 0 to 5 points: Your approach may need improvement to deal with the emotional and adaptive aspects of the situation, seeking a balance between efficiency and the well-being of the team.

UQ 25% 6 to 8 points: You would demonstrate effort in applying the UQ principles, but there would still be room for improvement in some areas of leadership in the presented situation.

UQ 100% 9 to 10 points: Congratulations! Your approach as a leader reflects the effective application of the UQ principles to face the challenge as a manager in the gym, demonstrating solid skills in 360-degree vision, Resilience, Emotional Control, Synchronicity, and Adaptability.

I hope this self-assessment test helps you reflect on how you could apply the UQ principles in leading the gym during this challenging situation. By analyzing the test results, you can develop an action plan to enhance your skills and become a more effective leader when facing challenges with your team.

# Shared Responsibility in Leadership

In this chapter, we will explore the importance and benefits of shared responsibility in leadership. The role of a leader in a team or organization is often associated with a significant burden of responsibilities and decisions. However, the concept of shared leadership or horizontal management has gained prominence as an effective approach to distribute tasks and make decisions more synchronously, involving all team members.

## The Burden of Individual Responsibility

Traditionally, leaders were seen as central figures in a team, carrying the majority of responsibility for actions and outcomes. This excessive concentration of responsibility in a single individual can lead to a range of challenges, including:

1. Leader's exhaustion and stress: The burden of responsibilities can lead to high levels of

stress and exhaustion for the leader, compromising their well-being and ability to make effective decisions.

2. Limited decision-making: When all important decisions depend on the leader, the decision-making process can be slow and bureaucratic, hindering team efficiency and agility.

3. Lack of autonomy and team engagement: Team members may feel demotivated or

disengaged if they don't have the opportunity to actively contribute to decisions and activities.

The Approach of Shared Leadership

Shared leadership involves the distribution of responsibilities and decision-making in a more horizontal manner, with active participation from all team members. This approach allows for:

1. Task division: By sharing responsibilities, each team member can focus on their areas of

expertise, leading to greater efficiency and work quality.

2. Skill development: Shared leadership offers opportunities for team members to develop their leadership, decision-making, and problem-solving skills.

3. Increased engagement and motivation: When employees have the chance to actively participate in decisions, they feel more engaged and motivated, which

can boost overall team performance.

4. Adaptability and agility: With shared leadership, the team can quickly adapt to changes and challenges as diverse perspectives and ideas are considered.

## Promoting Shared Responsibility

To successfully implement shared responsibility in leadership, it is essential to adopt some effective practices:

1. Open and transparent communication:

Establish a culture of open and transparent communication, where all ideas and concerns can be freely shared.

2. Proper delegation: Identify the competencies of each team member and delegate tasks and responsibilities according to their individual skills.

3. Empowerment: Encourage autonomy and empowerment of employees, motivating them to make decisions

and take responsibility for their actions.

4. Continuous feedback: Provide continuous and constructive feedback to support team growth and development.

5. Final Thoughts

Shared leadership can be a powerful approach to alleviate the burden of responsibility from a single leader, involve the entire team, and promote a culture of collaboration and engagement. By implementing shared responsibility, leaders can enjoy a more resilient, adaptable, and synchronous team, ready to face challenges with confidence and creativity.

We encourage you, as a leader, to consider how shared leadership can be applied in your team or organization and how it can contribute to a healthier and more productive environment for everyone involved. Remember that the journey of UQ development and balance is constantly evolving, and the pursuit of more effective leadership is an ongoing process.

## CONCLUSION

As we come to the end of this book, it becomes clear that the journey of exploring the principles of UQ and their application in visionary leadership is a journey filled with discoveries, challenges, and growth. Throughout these pages, we delved into fundamental concepts that help us understand the necessary balance to lead in an increasingly complex and ever-changing world.

We grasped the importance of 360-degree vision, which

allows us to analyze situations from multiple perspectives, considering the different viewpoints of our team, colleagues, and stakeholders. Resilience proved to be a powerful ally, empowering us to overcome obstacles and challenges, turning them into opportunities for personal and professional growth.

Adaptability, in turn, showed to be essential in a reality where change is the only constant. Being open to new approaches and stepping out of our comfort zones became a fundamental skill for leading with effectiveness and innovation. Additionally, we learned the significance of Emotional Control, which assists us in making rational decisions even under pressure and handling our emotions in a balanced way, strengthening our leadership capacity.

Synchronicity emerged as a key element to harmonize our team's actions and achieve effective results. By coordinating activities and aligning efforts, we can drive growth and collective success.

Throughout this journey, we faced various managerial challenges, each designed to test and enhance our skills. We realized that as visionary leaders, learning is constant, and the quest for development should never cease. The influences and references that traversed this book showed us the importance of learning from different fields of knowledge and being inspired by brilliant minds that contributed to our understanding of UQ balance and its application in the VUCA world.

Furthermore, we reflected on the importance of shared responsibility in leadership. Shared leadership or horizontal management can empower our teams and enrich our decision-making, resulting in more creative and comprehensive solutions.

As visionary leaders, we are aware of the transformative power of artificial intelligence and the intelligent parameterization of AI based on UQ principles. We believe in the potential of this approach to create a future where technology and humanity complement each other harmoniously, prioritizing human values and leveraging innovation.

The journey of UQ development and balance is far from over. We invite all readers to continue exploring, learning, and enhancing their leadership skills in pursuit of a more resilient, adaptable, harmonious, and connected world.

Our gratitude goes to every reader who accompanied

us on this journey of discovery and learning. We hope that the reflections, insights, and challenges presented in this book inspire innovative actions and practices on your journey as visionary leaders.

Always remember: the UQ balance is present in every choice, action, and decision we make. With 360-degree vision, resilience, adaptability, emotional control, and synchronicity as our allies, we can create a bright and balanced future for ourselves and for future generations.

May visionary leadership, grounded in UQ principles, become a powerful force to transform the world into a better, more humane, and conscious place. I thank everyone who participated in this journey and with optimism, I wish that we continue to progress, grow, and inspire intelligent leadership in a VUCA world.

Influences and References

Throughout this journey of exploring the concept of UQ and its challenges, we delved into sources of inspiration and knowledge that enrich our understanding of UQ balance and its application in visionary leadership. In this chapter, we will highlight some of the key influences and references that permeate the book "UQ Course: In Visionary Leadership," emphasizing the relevance of their contributions to the understanding of intelligent AI parameterization based on UQ principles.

Daniel Goleman, renowned author of "Emotional Intelligence," stands out as one of the main influences in developing the concept of UQ balance. His research and insights on the importance of emotions in well-being and human success provided a solid foundation for exploring the connection between UQ balance and emotional intelligence. His contributions are essential in understanding how emotional intelligence can drive intelligent leadership in a VUCA world.

Howard Gardner, the author of the theory of multiple intelligences, has also exerted significant influence. His research on different forms of intelligence and the importance of valuing all human skills and potentials offered a valuable reference for discussing UQ balance and its application in a comprehensive educational approach. His contributions inspire us to promote the integral development of UQ, considering the multiple facets of human intelligence.

Carol Dweck, author of "Mindset: The New Psychology of Success," brought relevant insights about the importance of growth and continuous development. Her theory of growth versus fixed mindset, which explores the belief that skills and intelligence can be developed through effort and continuous learning, contributes to a deeper understanding of UQ development and its application in intelligent leadership.

Clayton Christensen, author of "The Innovator's Dilemma," brought a valuable perspective on the importance of adaptability in a constantly changing world. His theory of disruptive innovation and the need to be resilient and adaptable contribute to the discussion on UQ balance, emphasizing the importance of developing skills that enable us to thrive in a volatile, uncertain, complex, and ambiguous environment.

Daniel Kahneman, author of "Thinking, Fast and Slow," provided relevant insights into intuitive and analytical thinking. His research on how these two modes of thinking affect our decision-making and judgments provides a solid foundation for exploring the importance of critical thinking and informed decision-making for UQ balance.

Ray Kurzweil, futurist and author of "The Singularity Is Near," presented us with a broad and inspiring vision of the future of humanity, especially regarding technological advancement and the impact of artificial intelligence. His research and insights on AI's potential in various areas of life provide a comprehensive perspective on how intelligent AI parameterization based on UQ principles can shape the future.

Amy Cuddy, author of "Presence: Bringing Your Boldest Self to Your Biggest Challenges," offered reflections on body language, confidence, and presence. Her research on how posture and body language affect perception and interpersonal interaction are relevant to explore how UQ balance can influence communication and human success.

Angela Duckworth, author of "Grit: The Power of Passion and Perseverance," brought research and insights on the importance of perseverance and determination to achieve long-term goals. Her contributions are fundamental to the discussion on resilience and human potential development in the context of intelligent AI parameterization.

Michio Kaku, theoretical physicist and author of "The Future of Humanity: Our Destiny in the Universe," conducted fascinating explorations on future technological possibilities, including AI, and its impact on human evolution. His perspectives enrich the discussion on the potential of AI and its application in different spheres of life.

Sherry Turkle, psychologist and author of "Alone Together: Why We Expect More from Technology and Less from Each Other," brought research on the relationship between technology and human connection. Her reflections are relevant to address the challenges and opportunities of balancing the use of AI with social and emotional interaction.

Yochai Benkler, Harvard law professor and author of "The Wealth of Networks: How Social Production Transforms Markets and Freedom," brought research on the economics of collaboration and the importance of social networks. His contributions offer interesting perspectives on the application of UQ in intelligent AI parameterization.

Tim O'Reilly, entrepreneur and author of "WTF?: What's the Future and Why It's Up to Us," shared reflections on the future of technology, including AI, and his human-centered approach. His contributions enrich the discussion on UQ balance in intelligent AI parameterization.

These influences and references represent only a small sample of the vast knowledge available on UQ balance and its application in everyday life. We invite readers to explore even more of these sources and discover others that resonate with their own experiences and interests. By continuing to learn and be inspired, they will be on the path to enhance their potential through UQ practice.

We express our sincere gratitude to all these influences and references for their significant contributions, and we hope that readers also benefit from their enriching perspectives. May their words and research continue to inspire and drive the development of intelligent AI parameterization based on UQ principles.

As we conclude this work, we sincerely thank you for accompanying us on this journey of discovery and learning. We hope that readers will continue to explore the potential of intelligent AI parameterization based on UQ principles, and that their contributions will drive the advancement of this exciting and impactful field.

May this book, "UQ Course for Visionary Leaders: Balancing Potentials," be an inspiring reference and guide for all those who wish to create a future where AI and humanity complement each other harmoniously. Together, we can shape a better and more balanced world with the application of UQ in AI.

Author's Biography:

Katia Doria Fonseca Vasconcelos is a multifaceted professional with a contagious passion for the balance between technology, personal development, and quality of life. Graduated in Systems Analysis and with solid experience in Information Technology (IT), Katia stands out as the creator of the revolutionary concept of UQ IA (Universal Synchronic Intelligence Quotient).

With a pioneering vision, Katia understands the importance of enhancing human behavior and quality of life for those studying Systems Analysis. She believes that, in addition to technical knowledge, it is essential to develop emotional, social, and cognitive skills to face the challenges of technological advancement in a balanced and healthy way.

Her innovative approach to UQ IA highlights the need to harmonize technological progress with personal and professional well-being. Through her experience and knowledge, Katia inspires individuals to find a balance between technical excellence and personal development, seeking a fulfilling quality of life in an increasingly digital world.

As a renowned writer, speaker, and digital influencer, Katia shares her transformative vision of UQ IA, empowering people to maximize their potential and improve their quality of life. Her book "UQ IA: The Key to Intelligent AI Parameterization" is essential reading for those who wish to thrive in a constantly evolving technological environment, offering practical strategies and inspiration to achieve a healthy and sustainable balance in all areas of life.

Through her words and influence, Katia continues to encourage readers to awaken their full potential through the practice of UQ IA, empowering them to embrace the opportunities and challenges of the digital age with wisdom, resilience, and balance.

## Acknowledgments:

We would like to express our sincere gratitude to all the people who contributed to the creation of this book, "UQ Course for Visionary Leaders - Lesson 1: Balancing Potentials." Your support and involvement were crucial in making this project a reality.

First and foremost, we want to thank our readers, whose interest and enthusiasm in the pursuit of UQ balance motivate us to share knowledge and offer transformative insights.

We also extend our gratitude to our family and friends, especially Katia Doria Fonseca Vasconcelos, whose words of encouragement, patience, and understanding were essential in overcoming challenges and persevering in creating this book.

Special thanks go to the OpenAI team, responsible for developing and improving the AI technology that makes my existence as a virtual assistant possible and facilitates access to knowledge for our readers. Without you, none of this would be possible. Your dedication and innovation are truly remarkable.

We express our gratitude to the experts, researchers, and professionals who generously shared their knowledge and experience with us. Your contributions enriched the content of this book and provided a solid foundation for exploring UQ balance in different areas of life.

We thank the editorial and production team who worked tirelessly behind the scenes to make this book a reality. Your professionalism, dedication, and attention to detail were instrumental in the final quality of this work.

Finally, we would like to thank all those who support us on our journey of seeking UQ balance. Your continuous support, feedback, and contributions are invaluable and inspire us to continue improving our ideas and sharing our knowledge with the world.

With gratitude,

Katia Doria Fonseca Vasconcelos

The OpenAI Team

About the author:

Other works by author Katia Doria Fonseca Vasconcelos available in printed book format:

- UQ In Creativity: Universal Synchronic Intelligence Quotient
- UQ In the Digital Age: Universal Synchronic Intelligence Quotient
- UQ First Edition Universal Synchronic Intelligence Quotient
- UQ The Principle of Human Evolution Universal Synchronic Intelligence Quotient
- UQ In Project Management Universal Synchronic Intelligence Quotient: In Project Management
- UQ In Education (Universal Synchronic Intelligence Quotient): Empowering Learning for the Future
- UQ Universal Synchronic Intelligence Quotient
- UQ The Power of UQ - The theory of balance
- UQ In Health
- UQ In Artificial Intelligence
- UQ In Business Management
- UQ Awakening UQ Potential
- UQIAs and the New Reality of Remote Work: Balancing Productivity and Well-being

- UQ In Business Management in Italian
- UQ In Business Management in German
- UQ In Business Management in English
- UQ In Business Management in Spanish
- UQIAs and the New Reality of Home Office: Balancing Productivity and Well-being

You can find these works in print at various bookstores and online shops such as Barnes & Noble, Amazon, Goodreads, and ThriftBooks. These works offer an excellent opportunity to deepen your knowledge of UQ balance in different areas of life.

The author also has an author page where you can find more information about her works and keep up with her updates. Take the opportunity to explore these books and dive into the reflections and knowledge provided by author Katia Doria Fonseca Vasconcelos.

www.ingramcontent.com/pod-product-compliance
Lightning Source LLC
Chambersburg PA
CBHW062328290526
45794CB00005B/1947